make it yourself

salads

make it yourself

salads

LOVE
FOOD

This edition published in 2009
Love Food ® is an imprint of Parragon Books Ltd

Parragon
Queen Street House
4 Queen Street
Bath BA1 1HE, UK

Cover design by Talking Design
Photography by Günter Beer
Food styling by Stefan Paul

ISBN: 978-1-4075-8024-1

Printed in China

Notes for the reader
• This book uses imperial, metric, and US cup measurements. Follow the same units
of measurement throughout; do not mix imperial and metric. All spoon measurements
are level: teaspoons are assumed to be 5 ml, and tablespoons are assumed to be 15 ml.
Unless otherwise stated, milk is assumed to be whole, eggs and individual vegetables
such as potatoes are medium, and pepper is freshly ground black pepper.
• The times given are an approximate guide only. Preparation times differ according
to the techniques used by different people and the cooking times may also vary from
those given as a result of the type of oven used. Optional ingredients, variations or
serving suggestions have not been included in the calculations.
• Recipes using raw or very lightly cooked eggs should be avoided by infants, the
elderly, pregnant women, convalescents, and anyone with a chronic condition.
Pregnant and breastfeeding women are advised to avoid eating peanuts and peanut
products. Sufferers from nut allergies should be aware that some of the ready-prepared
ingredients used in the recipes in this book may contain nuts. Always check the
packaging before use.

Contents

Introduction

Today, salads are one of the ultimate health foods. They can contain an exciting variety of colorful, delicious and satisfying ingredients that provide the nutrients essential for healthy living. We are all being urged to eat more fruit and vegetables every day, and a salad a day can go a long way to helping toward those all important recommendations. With fresh produce from all corners of the globe readily available in supermarkets and gourmet food stores, you can enjoy a variety of salads all year round but, remember, salads are at their most flavorsome and nutritious when made with seasonal produce in its prime.

If you regularly fall back on the old favorite of just tossing a few green leaves with a simple oil-and-vinegar dressing, it's definitely time to think again. It's very easy to mix and match ingredients and the choice has never been greater. And don't make the mistake of thinking all salad ingredients have to be raw, either. Adding small amounts of cooked meat, poultry and seafood to salad leaves and other vegetables gives you a satisfying meal, as the recipes inside this book demonstrate.

Colorful greens

Even with so many ingredients to choose from, salad greens still provide the backbone of many popular salads. Take a look around your supermarket and you'll see leaves in many colors and textures. They also have a variety of flavors, from robust and peppery to sweet, nutty, and mild. The greater the variety of leaves you include in your salad, the more interesting it will be, and the

more nutrients it will contain. When you select salad leaves, remember that the darker colored ones, such as spinach leaves, contain more beta-carotene, which helps fight some forms of cancer and other illnesses. Leafy green vegetables are also excellent sources of fiber.

Keep it fresh

Good salads are only made with good ingredients, and freshness is all-important when buying salad greens. Because of the leaves' high water content, they are very perishable, so buy them as close as possible to serving. Not only will they taste best, but they contain the most nutrients when they are in peak condition, Let your eyes guide you when shopping for salad greens—fresh leaves look fresh. They won't have any leaves tinged with brown, nor will they be wilted or slimy. When you get salad

ingredients home, give them a rinse in cold water, then spin them dry or use a tea cloth to pat them dry. Never leave them to soak in a sink of cold water because all the water soluble vitamins and minerals will leech out. Use leafy greens as soon as possible, but most will keep for up to four days in a sealed container in the refrigerator. Once you open bags of prepared leaves, however, they should be used within 24 hours. You can prepare salad greens several hours in advance and store in the refrigerator, but do not dress until just before serving, because the acid in most dressings causes the leaves to wilt and become unappetizing.

Classic
Salads

serves 4

10 oz/280 g buffalo
mozzarella, drained and
thinly sliced

8 tomatoes, sliced

20 fresh basil leaves

1/2 cup extra virgin olive oil

salt and pepper

three-color salad

Arrange the mozzarella and tomato slices on 4 individual serving plates and season to taste with salt. Set aside in a cool place for 30 minutes.

Sprinkle the basil leaves over the salad and drizzle with the olive oil. Season with pepper and serve immediately.

serves 4

3¹/2 oz/100 g mixed salad greens, such as looseleaf lettuce, baby spinach, and arugula

1 lb 2 oz/500 g mozzarella cheese, sliced

for the dressing

5 oz/140 g sun-dried tomatoes in olive oil (drained weight), reserving the oil from the jar

1/4 cup coarsely shredded fresh basil

1/4 cup coarsely chopped fresh flat-leaf parsley

1 tbsp capers, rinsed

1 tbsp balsamic vinegar

1 garlic clove, coarsely chopped

extra olive oil, if necessary

pepper

mozzarella salad with sun-dried tomatoes

Put the sun-dried tomatoes, basil, parsley, capers, vinegar, and garlic in a food processor or blender. Measure the oil from the sun-dried tomatoes jar and make it up to 2/3 cup with more olive oil if necessary. Add it to the food processor or blender and process until smooth. Season to taste with pepper.

Divide the salad greens among 4 individual serving plates. Top with the slices of mozzarella and spoon the dressing over them. Serve immediately.

serves 4

8 oz/225 g asparagus spears

1 lamb's lettuce, washed and torn

1 handful arugula or mizuna leaves

1 lb/450 g ripe tomatoes, sliced

12 black olives, pitted and chopped

1 tbsp toasted pine nuts

for the dressing

1 tsp lemon oil

1 tbsp olive oil

1 tsp whole grain mustard

2 tbsp balsamic vinegar

sea salt and pepper

asparagus & tomato salad

Steam the asparagus spears for 8 minutes, or until tender. Rinse under cold running water to prevent them cooking any further, then cut into 2-inch/5-cm pieces.

Arrange the lettuce and arugula leaves around a salad platter to form the base of the salad. Place the sliced tomatoes in a circle on top and the asparagus in the center.

Sprinkle the black olives and pine nuts over the top. Put the lemon oil, olive oil, mustard, and vinegar in a screw-top jar and season to taste with sea salt and black pepper. Shake vigorously and drizzle over the salad.

serves 4

2 tbsp olive oil

2 tsp cumin seeds

2 garlic cloves, crushed

2 tsp grated fresh ginger

1$^1/_2$ cups split red lentils

3 cups vegetable stock

2 tbsp chopped fresh mint

2 tbsp chopped fresh cilantro

2 red onions, thinly sliced

4$^3/_8$ cups baby spinach leaves

1 tsp hazelnut oil

5$^1/_2$ oz/150 g soft goat cheese

4 tbsp plain yogurt

pepper

warm red lentil salad with goat cheese

Heat half the olive oil in a large pan over medium heat, add the cumin seeds, garlic, and ginger and cook for 2 minutes, stirring constantly.

Stir in the lentils, then add the stock, a ladleful at a time, until it is all absorbed, stirring constantly—this will take about 20 minutes. Remove from the heat and stir in the herbs.

Meanwhile, heat the remaining olive oil in a skillet over medium heat, add the onions, and cook, stirring frequently, for 10 minutes, or until soft and lightly browned.

Toss the spinach in the hazelnut oil in a bowl, then divide among 4 serving plates.

Mash the goat cheese with the yogurt in a small bowl and season to taste with pepper.

Divide the lentils among the serving plates and top with the onions and goat cheese mixture.

serves 4

3 tbsp pine nuts

2 red onions, chopped

4 tbsp olive oil

2 garlic cloves, crushed

3 slices whole wheat bread, cubed

7 oz/200 g mixed salad greens

9 oz/250 g cremini mushrooms, sliced

5½ oz/150 g shiitake mushrooms, sliced

5½ oz/150 g oyster mushrooms, torn

for the dressing

1 garlic clove, crushed

2 tbsp red wine vinegar

4 tbsp walnut oil

1 tbsp finely chopped fresh parsley

pepper

mixed mushroom salad

Preheat the oven to 350°F/180°C. Heat a nonstick skillet over medium heat, add the pine nuts, and cook, turning, until just browned. Tip into a bowl and set aside.

Put the onions and 1 tablespoon of the olive oil into a roasting pan and toss to coat. Roast in the preheated oven for 30 minutes.

Meanwhile, heat 1 tablespoon of the remaining oil with the garlic in the nonstick skillet over high heat. Add the bread and cook, turning frequently, for 5 minutes, or until brown and crisp. Remove from the skillet and set aside.

Divide the salad greens among 4 serving plates and add the roasted onions. To make the dressing, whisk together the garlic, vinegar, and oil in a small bowl. Stir in the parsley and season to taste with pepper. Drizzle over the salad and onions.

Heat the remaining oil in a skillet, add the cremini and shiitake mushrooms, and cook for 2–3 minutes, stirring frequently. Add the oyster mushrooms and cook for an additional 2–3 minutes. Divide the hot mushroom mixture among the 4 plates. Sprinkle over the pine nuts and croutons and serve.

serves 4

2 ripe tomatoes

3¹/₂ oz/100 g mozzarella cheese

2 avocados

few fresh basil leaves, torn into pieces

20 black olives

fresh crusty bread, to serve

for the dressing

1 tbsp olive oil

1¹/₂ tbsp white wine vinegar

1 tsp coarse grain mustard

salt and pepper

tomato, mozzarella & avocado salad

Using a sharp knife, cut the tomatoes into thick wedges and place in a large serving dish. Drain the mozzarella cheese and coarsely tear into pieces. Cut the avocados in half and remove the pits. Cut the flesh into slices, then arrange the mozzarella cheese and avocado with the tomatoes.

To make the dressing, mix together the oil, vinegar, and mustard in a small bowl, add salt and pepper to taste, then drizzle over the salad.

Sprinkle the basil and olives over the top and serve at once with fresh crusty bread.

serves 4

8 oz/225 g dried conchiglie

1³/₄ oz/50 g pine nuts

12 oz/350 g cherry tomatoes,
cut in half

1 red bell pepper, seeded and
cut into bite-size chunks

1 red onion, chopped

7 oz/200 g buffalo
mozzarella, cubed

12 black olives, pitted

1 oz/25 g fresh basil leaves

shavings of fresh Parmesan
cheese, to garnish

crusty bread, to serve

for the dressing

5 tbsp extra virgin olive oil

2 tbsp balsamic vinegar

1 tbsp chopped fresh basil

salt and pepper

italian salad

Bring a large pan of lightly salted water to a boil. Add the pasta and cook over medium heat for about 10 minutes, or according to the package instructions. When cooked, the pasta should be tender but still firm to the bite. Drain, rinse under cold running water, and drain again. Let cool.

While the pasta is cooking, put the pine nuts in a dry skillet and cook over low heat for 1–2 minutes, until golden brown. Remove from the heat, transfer to a dish, and let cool.

To make the dressing, put the oil, vinegar, and basil into a small bowl. Season with salt and pepper and stir together well. Cover with plastic wrap and set to one side.

To assemble the salad, divide the pasta among serving bowls. Add the pine nuts, tomatoes, red bell pepper, onion, cheese, and olives. Scatter over the basil leaves, then drizzle over the dressing. Garnish with fresh Parmesan cheese shavings and serve with crusty bread.

serves 4

7 oz/200 g feta cheese

1/2 head of Webbs lettuce or
1 lettuce such as romaine or
escarole, shredded or sliced

4 tomatoes, cut into quarters

1/2 cucumber, sliced

12 Greek black olives, pitted

2 tbsp chopped fresh herbs,
such as oregano, flat-leaf
parsley, mint, or basil

for the dressing

6 tbsp extra virgin olive oil

2 tbsp fresh lemon juice

1 garlic clove, crushed

pinch of sugar

salt and pepper

greek salad

Make the dressing by whisking together the oil, lemon juice, garlic, sugar, salt, and pepper, in a small bowl. Set aside. Cut the feta cheese into cubes about 1 inch/2.5 cm square. Put the lettuce, tomatoes, and cucumber in a salad bowl. Scatter over the cheese and toss together.

Just before serving, whisk the dressing, pour over the salad greens, and toss together. Scatter over the olives and chopped herbs and serve.

serves 4

3/8 cup Puy lentils

1 lb/450 g new potatoes

6 scallions

1 tbsp olive oil

2 tbsp balsamic vinegar

salt and pepper

warm new potato & lentil salad

Bring a large pan of water to a boil. Rinse the lentils, then cook for 20 minutes, or until tender. Drain and rinse, then put to one side.

Meanwhile, steam or boil the potatoes until they are soft right through. Drain and halve.

Trim the base from the scallions and cut them in slices.

Put the lentils, potatoes, and scallions into a serving dish and toss with the olive oil and vinegar. Season with plenty of black pepper and a little salt if required.

serves 4

2/3 cup olive oil

2 garlic cloves

5 slices white bread, crusts removed, cut into 1/2-inch/1-cm cubes

1 large egg

2 romaine lettuces or 3 Boston lettuces

2 tbsp lemon juice

8 canned anchovy fillets, drained and coarsely chopped

3/4 cup fresh Parmesan cheese shavings

salt and pepper

caesar salad

Bring a small, heavy-bottom pan of water to a boil.

Meanwhile, heat 4 tablespoons of the olive oil in a heavy-bottom skillet. Add the garlic and cubed bread and cook, stirring and tossing frequently, for 4–5 minutes, or until the bread is crispy and golden all over. Remove from the skillet with a slotted spoon and drain on paper towels.

Add the egg to the boiling water and cook for 1 minute, then remove from the pan and set aside.

Arrange the salad greens in a salad bowl. Mix together the remaining olive oil and lemon juice, then season to taste with salt and pepper. Crack the egg into the dressing and whisk to blend. Pour the dressing over the salad greens, toss well, then add the croutons and chopped anchovies and toss the salad again. Sprinkle with Parmesan cheese shavings and serve.

Meat & Poultry Salads

serves 4

1 lb 2 oz/500 g red dessert apples, diced

3 tbsp fresh lemon juice

2/3 cup light mayonnaise

1 head celery

4 shallots, sliced

1 garlic clove, finely chopped

3/4 cup walnuts, chopped

1 lb 2 oz/500 g cooked chicken, cubed

1 cos lettuce

pepper

chopped walnuts, to garnish

waldorf summer chicken salad

Place the apples in a bowl with the lemon juice and 1 tablespoon of mayonnaise. Leave for 40 minutes.

Using a sharp knife, slice the celery very thinly. Add the celery, shallots, garlic, and walnuts to the apple and mix together. Stir in the remaining mayonnaise and blend thoroughly.

Add the cooked chicken to the bowl and mix well.

Line a serving dish with the lettuce. Pile the chicken salad into a serving bowl, sprinkle with pepper and garnish with the chopped walnuts.

serves 4

5 1/2 oz/150 g arugula leaves

2 celery stalks, trimmed and sliced

1/2 cucumber, sliced

2 scallions, trimmed and sliced

2 tbsp chopped fresh parsley

1 oz/25 g walnut pieces

12 oz/350 g boneless roast chicken, sliced

4 1/2 oz/125 g bleu cheese, cubed

handful of seedless red grapes, cut in half (optional)

salt and pepper

for the dressing

2 tbsp olive oil

1 tbsp sherry vinegar

1 tsp Dijon mustard

1 tbsp chopped mixed herbs

chicken, cheese & arugula salad

Wash the arugula leaves, pat dry with paper towels, and put them into a large salad bowl. Add the celery, cucumber, scallions, parsley, and walnuts and mix together well. Transfer onto a large serving platter. Arrange the chicken slices over the salad, then scatter over the cheese. Add the red grapes, if using. Season well with salt and pepper.

To make the dressing, put all the ingredients into a screw-top jar and shake well. Alternatively, put them into a bowl and mix together well. Drizzle the dressing over the salad and serve.

serves 4

14 oz/400 g small new potatoes, scrubbed and cut in half, lengthwise

7 oz/200 g baby corn cobs

1¹/₂ cups bean sprouts

3 scallions, trimmed and sliced

4 cooked, skinless chicken breasts, sliced

1 tbsp chopped lemongrass

2 tbsp chopped fresh cilantro

salt and pepper

wedges of lime, to garnish

fresh cilantro leaves, to garnish

for the dressing

6 tbsp chili oil or sesame oil

2 tbsp lime juice

1 tbsp light soy sauce

1 tbsp chopped fresh cilantro

1 small, red chile, seeded and finely sliced

thai-style chicken salad

Bring two pans of water to the boil. Put the potatoes into one pan and cook for 15 minutes until tender. Put the corn cobs into the other pan and cook for 5 minutes until tender. Drain the potatoes and corn cobs well and let cool.

When the vegetables are cool, transfer them into a large serving dish. Add the bean sprouts, scallions, chicken, lemongrass, and cilantro and season with salt and pepper.

To make the dressing, put all the ingredients into a screw-top jar and shake well. Alternatively, put them into a bowl and mix together well. Drizzle the dressing over the salad and garnish with lime wedges and cilantro leaves. Serve at once.

serves 4

4 cups chicken stock

scant 1 cup mixed long-grain and wild rice

2 tbsp corn oil

8 oz/225 g skinless, boneless turkey breast, trimmed of all visible fat and cut into thin strips

2 cups snow peas

4 oz/115 g oyster mushrooms, torn into pieces

1/4 cup shelled pistachio nuts, finely chopped

2 tbsp chopped fresh cilantro

1 tbsp snipped fresh garlic chives

1 tbsp balsamic vinegar

salt and pepper

fresh garlic chives, to garnish

turkey & rice salad

Set aside 3 tablespoons of the chicken stock and bring the remainder to a boil in a large pan. Add the rice and cook for 30 minutes, or until tender. Drain and let cool slightly.

Meanwhile, heat 1 tablespoon of the oil in a preheated wok or skillet. Stir-fry the turkey over medium heat for 3–4 minutes, or until cooked through. Using a slotted spoon, transfer the turkey to a dish. Add the snow peas and mushrooms to the wok and stir-fry for 1 minute. Add the reserved stock, bring to a boil, then reduce the heat, cover, and let simmer for 3–4 minutes. Transfer the vegetables to the dish and let cool slightly.

Thoroughly mix together the rice, turkey, snow peas, mushrooms, nuts, cilantro, and garlic chives, then season to taste with salt and pepper. Drizzle with the remaining corn oil and the vinegar and garnish with fresh garlic chives. Serve warm.

serves 4

12 oz/350 g boneless duck breasts

2 tbsp all-purpose flour

1 egg

2 tbsp water

2 tbsp sesame seeds

3 tbsp sesame oil

1/2 head Chinese cabbage, shredded

3 celery stalks, finely sliced

8 radishes, trimmed and halved

salt and pepper

fresh basil leaves, to garnish

for the dressing

finely grated peel of 1 lime

2 tbsp lime juice

2 tbsp olive oil

1 tbsp light soy sauce

1 tbsp chopped fresh basil

salt and pepper

duck & radish salad

Put each duck breast among sheets of baking parchment or plastic wrap. Use a meat mallet or rolling pin to beat them out and flatten them slightly.

Sprinkle the flour onto a large plate and season with salt and pepper. Beat the egg and water together in a shallow bowl, then sprinkle the sesame seeds onto a separate plate.

Dip the duck breasts first into the seasoned flour, then into the egg mixture and finally into the sesame seeds, to coat the duck evenly. Heat the sesame oil in a preheated wok or large skillet.

Fry the duck breasts over medium heat for about 8 minutes, turning once. To test whether they are cooked, insert a sharp knife into the thickest part—the juices should run clear. Lift them out and drain on paper towels.

To make the dressing for the salad, whisk together the lime peel and juice, olive oil, soy sauce, and chopped basil. Season with a little salt and pepper.

Arrange the Chinese cabbage, celery, and radishes on a serving plate. Slice the duck breasts thinly and place on top of the salad. Drizzle with the dressing and garnish with fresh basil leaves. Serve at once.

serves 4

4 tenderloin steaks, about
4 oz/115 g each, fat discarded

2 tbsp red wine vinegar

2 tbsp orange juice

2 tsp prepared English
mustard

6 oz/175 g new potatoes

4 oz/115 g green beans,
trimmed

6 oz/175 g mixed salad
greens, such as baby spinach,
arugula, and mizuna

1 yellow bell pepper, seeded,
peeled, and cut into strips

6 oz/175 g cherry tomatoes,
halved

black olives, pitted (optional)

2 tsp extra virgin olive oil

warm beef niçoise

Place the steaks in a shallow dish. Blend the vinegar with
1 tablespoon of orange juice and 1 teaspoon of mustard. Pour over
the steaks, cover, then let stand in the refrigerator for at least
30 minutes. Turn over halfway through the marinating time.

Meanwhile, place the potatoes in a pan and cover with cold
water. Bring to a boil, then cover and let simmer for 15 minutes,
or until tender when pierced with a fork. Drain and set aside.

Bring a saucepan of water to the boil, add the beans and cook for
5 minutes, or until just tender. Drain, plunge into cold water and
drain again. Arrange the potatoes and beans on top of the salad
leaves together with the bell pepper, cherry tomatoes, and olives,
if using. Blend the remaining orange juice and mustard with the
olive oil and set aside.

Heat a stovetop grill pan until smoking. Drain the steaks and
cook for 3–5 minutes on each side or according to personal
preference. Slice the steaks and arrange on top of the salad, then
pour over the dressing and serve.

serves 4

1 lb 10 oz/750 g beef fillet, trimmed of any visible fat

2 tsp Worcestershire sauce

3 tbsp olive oil

14 oz/400 g green beans

3^{1}/$_{2}$ oz/100 g small pasta, such as orecchiette

2 red onions, finely sliced

1 large head radicchio

generous ^{1}/$_{4}$ cup green olives, pitted

scant ^{1}/$_{3}$ cup shelled hazelnuts, whole

pepper

for the dressing

1 tsp Dijon mustard

2 tbsp white wine vinegar

5 tbsp olive oil

roast beef salad

Preheat the oven to 425°F/220°C. Rub the beef with pepper to taste and Worcestershire sauce. Heat 2 tablespoons of the oil in a small roasting pan over high heat, add the beef, and sear on all sides. Transfer the dish to the preheated oven and roast for 30 minutes. Remove and let cool.

Bring a large pan of water to a boil, add the beans, and cook for 5 minutes, or until just tender. Remove with a slotted spoon and refresh the beans under cold running water. Drain and put into a large bowl.

Return the bean cooking water to a boil, add the pasta, and cook for 11 minutes, or until tender. Drain, return to the pan, and toss with the remaining oil.

Add the pasta to the beans with the onions, radicchio leaves, olives, and hazelnuts, mix gently and transfer to a serving bowl or dish. Arrange some thinly sliced beef on top.

Whisk together the dressing ingredients in a separate bowl, then pour over the salad and serve at once with extra sliced beef.

serves 4

2 tbsp sunflower oil, plus extra for broiling the lamb

1 tbsp tomato paste

1/2 tbsp ground cumin

1 tsp lemon juice

1 garlic clove, crushed

pinch of cayenne pepper

1 lb 2 oz/500 g lamb neck fillets, trimmed, with excess fat removed

salt and pepper

toasted sesame seeds and chopped fresh parsley, to garnish

for the dressing

2 tbsp fresh lemon juice

1 tsp honey

3 oz/75 g thick plain yogurt

2 tbsp finely shredded fresh mint

2 tbsp chopped fresh parsley

1 tbsp finely snipped fresh chives

salt and pepper

broiled lamb with yogurt & herb dressing

Mix together the oil, tomato paste, cumin, lemon juice, garlic, cayenne and salt and pepper to taste in a non-metallic bowl. Add the lamb and rub all over with the marinade. Cover the bowl and marinate in the refrigerator for at least 2 hours, but ideally overnight.

Meanwhile, to make the dressing, whisk together the lemon juice and honey until the honey dissolves. Whisk in the yogurt until well blended. Stir in the herbs and add salt and pepper to taste. Cover and chill until required.

Remove the lamb from the fridge 15 minutes before you are ready to cook. Heat the broiler to its highest setting and lightly brush the broiler rack with oil. Broil the lamb, turning it once, for 10 minutes for medium and 12 minutes for well done. Leave the lamb to cool completely, then cover and chill until required.

Thinly slice the lamb, then divide among 4 plates. Adjust the seasoning in the dressing, if necessary, then spoon over the lamb slices. Sprinkle with toasted sesame seeds and parsley and serve.

serves 4-6

1 small pumpkin, about
3^1/$_2$lb/1.6 kg

2 red onions, cut into wedges

olive oil

3^1/$_2$ oz/100 g green beans,
topped and tailed and cut in
half

1^1/$_4$ lb/600 g roast pork, any
skin or rind removed and cut
into bite-size chunks

large handful fresh arugula
leaves

3^1/$_2$ oz/100 g feta cheese,
drained and crumbled

2 tbsp toasted pine nuts

2 tbsp chopped fresh parsley

salt and pepper

for the vinaigrette

6 tbsp extra virgin olive oil

3 tbsp balsamic vinegar

^{1}/$_2$ tsp sugar

^{1}/$_2$ tsp Dijon, prepared
English or whole grain
mustard

salt and pepper

roast pork & pumpkin salad

Preheat the oven to 400°F/200°C. Cut the pumpkin in half, scoop out the seeds and fibers and cut the flesh into wedges about 1½ inches/4 cm wide. Very lightly rub the pumpkin and onion wedges with the olive oil, place in a roasting pan and roast for 25–30 minutes until the pumpkin and onions are tender but holding their shape.

Meanwhile, bring a small pan of salted water to a boil. Add the green beans and blanch for 5 minutes, or until tender. Drain well and cool under cold running water to stop the cooking. Drain well and pat dry.

Remove the pumpkin and onion wedges from the oven as soon as they are tender and leave to cool completely. When the pumpkin is cool, peel and cut into bite-size pieces.

To make the vinaigrette, put the oil, vinegar, sugar, mustard, and salt and pepper to taste into a screw-top jar and shake until blended.

To assemble the salad, put the pumpkins, onions, beans, pork, arugula, feta, pine nuts, and parsley in a large bowl and gently toss together—be careful not to break up the pumpkin. Shake the dressing again, pour over the salad and gently toss. Divide among individual bowls and serve.

serves 4

generous 6 cups fresh baby
spinach leaves

2 tbsp olive oil

5¹/₂ oz/150 g pancetta

10 oz/280 g mixed wild
mushrooms, sliced

for the dressing

5 tbsp olive oil

1 tbsp balsamic vinegar

1 tsp Dijon mustard

pinch of sugar

salt and pepper

warm mushroom, spinach & pancetta salad

To make the dressing, place the olive oil, vinegar, mustard, sugar, salt, and pepper in a small bowl and whisk together.

Rinse the baby spinach under cold running water, then drain and place in a large salad bowl.

Heat the oil in a large skillet. Add the pancetta and cook for 3 minutes. Add the mushrooms and cook for 3–4 minutes, or until tender.

Pour the dressing into the skillet and immediately turn the cooked mixture and dressing into the bowl with the spinach. Toss until coated with the dressing and serve at once.

3

Fish & Seafood Salads

serves 4

2 tuna steaks, about 3/4 inch/2 cm thick

olive oil, for brushing

9 oz/250 g green beans, trimmed

1/2 cup vinaigrette or garlic vinaigrette dressing

2 hearts of lettuce, leaves separated

3 large hard-cooked eggs, cut into quarters

2 tomatoes, cut into wedges

1 3/4 oz/50 g anchovy fillets in oil, drained

2 oz/55 g Niçoise olives, pitted

salt and pepper

salad niçoise

Heat a ridged cast-iron grill pan over high heat, until you can feel the heat rising from the surface. Brush the tuna steaks with oil, place oiled side down on the hot pan, and cook for 2 minutes. Lightly brush the top sides of the tuna steaks with more oil. Use a pair of tongs to turn the tuna steaks over, then season to taste with salt and pepper. Continue cooking for another 2 minutes for rare or up to 4 minutes for well done. Let cool.

Meanwhile, bring a pan of salted water to a boil. Add the beans to the pan and return to a boil, then boil for 3 minutes, or until tender-crisp. Drain the beans and immediately transfer them to a large bowl. Pour over the vinaigrette and stir together, then let the beans cool in the dressing.

To serve, line a platter with lettuce leaves. Lift the beans out of the bowl, leaving the excess dressing behind, and pile them in the center of the platter. Break the tuna into large pieces and arrange it over the beans. Arrange the hard-cooked eggs and the tomatoes around the side. Arrange the anchovy fillets over the salad, then scatter with the olives. Drizzle the remaining dressing in the bowl over everything and serve.

serves 4

7 oz/200 g dried fusilli

1 red bell pepper, seeded and
quartered

1 red onion, sliced

4 tomatoes, sliced

7 oz/200 g canned tuna in
brine, drained and flaked

for the dressing

6 tbsp basil-flavored oil or
extra virgin olive oil

3 tbsp white wine vinegar

1 tbsp lime juice

1 tsp mustard

1 tsp honey

4 tbsp chopped fresh basil,
plus extra sprigs to garnish

tuna & herbed fusilli salad

Bring a large pan of lightly salted water to a boil. Add the pasta, return to a boil, and cook for 8–10 minutes until tender but still firm to the bite.

Meanwhile, put the bell pepper quarters under a broiler preheated to hot and cook for 10–12 minutes until the skins begin to blacken. Transfer to a plastic bag, seal, and set aside.

Remove the pasta from the heat, drain, and set aside to cool. Remove the bell pepper quarters from the bag and peel off the skins. Slice the bell pepper into strips.

To make the dressing, put all the dressing ingredients in a large bowl and stir together well. Add the pasta, bell pepper strips, onion, tomatoes, and tuna. Toss together gently, then divide among serving bowls. Garnish with basil sprigs and serve.

serves 4

8 oz/225 g trout fillets

8 oz/225 g white fish fillets

1¼ cups water

1 stem lemongrass

2 lime leaves

1 large red chile

1 bunch scallions, trimmed and shredded

4 oz/115 g fresh pineapple flesh, diced

1 small red bell pepper, seeded and diced

1 bunch watercress, washed and trimmed

fresh snipped chives, to garnish

for the dressing

1 tbsp sunflower oil

1 tbsp rice wine vinegar

pinch of chili powder

1 tsp clear honey

salt and pepper

sweet & sour fish salad

Rinse the fish, place in a skillet and pour over the water. Bend the lemongrass in half to bruise it and add to the skillet with the lime leaves. Prick the chile with a fork and add to the pan. Bring to a boil and simmer for 7–8 minutes. Let cool.

Drain the fish fillet thoroughly, then flake the flesh away from the skin and place it in a bowl. Gently stir in the scallions, pineapple and bell pepper.

Arrange the washed watercress on 4 serving plates and spoon the cooked fish mixture on top.

To make the dressing, mix together all the ingredients, seasoning well. Spoon the dressing over the fish and serve the salad garnished with chives.

serves 4

1³/4 oz/50 g wild arugula
leaves

1 tbsp chopped fresh flat-leaf
parsley

2 scallions, finely diced

2 large avocados

1 tbsp lemon juice

9 oz/250 g smoked salmon

for the dressing

2/3 cup mayonnaise

2 tbsp lime juice

finely grated rind of 1 lime

1 tbsp chopped fresh flat-leaf
parsley, plus extra sprigs
to garnish

smoked salmon & wild arugula salad

Shred the arugula and arrange in 4 individual glass bowls. Sprinkle over the chopped parsley and scallions.

Halve, peel, and pit the avocados and cut into thin slices or small chunks. Brush with the lemon juice to prevent discoloration, then divide among the salad bowls. Mix together gently. Cut the smoked salmon into strips and sprinkle over the top.

Put the mayonnaise in a bowl, then add the lime juice, lime rind, and chopped parsley. Mix together well. Spoon some of the mayonnaise dressing on top of each salad and garnish with parsley sprigs.

serves 4

1 lb/450 g new potatoes

4 salmon steaks, about 4 oz/115 g each

1 avocado

juice of 1/2 lemon

2 oz/55 g baby spinach leaves

4 1/2 oz/125 g mixed small salad leaves, including watercress

12 cherry tomatoes, halved

2 oz/55 g chopped walnuts

for the dressing

3 tbsp unsweetened clear apple juice

1 tsp balsamic vinegar

freshly ground black pepper

salmon & avocado salad

Cut the new potatoes into bite-sized pieces, put into a saucepan and cover with cold water. Bring to the boil, then reduce the heat, cover and simmer for 10–15 minutes, or until just tender. Drain and keep warm.

Meanwhile, preheat the broiler to medium. Cook the salmon steaks under the preheated broiler for 10–15 minutes, depending on the thickness of the steaks, turning halfway through cooking. Remove from the broiler and keep warm.

While the potatoes and salmon are cooking, cut the avocado in half, remove and discard the pit and peel the flesh. Cut the avocado flesh into slices and coat in the lemon juice to prevent discoloration.

Toss together the spinach leaves and mixed salad leaves in a large serving bowl until combined, then divide among 4 serving plates. Arrange 6 cherry tomato halves on each plate of salad.

Remove and discard the skin and any bones from the salmon. Flake the salmon and divide among the plates along with the potatoes. Sprinkle the walnuts over the salads.

To make the dressing, mix the apple juice and vinegar together in a small bowl or jug and season well with pepper. Drizzle over the salads and serve immediately.

serves 4

large handful of mixed
lettuce leaves

12 cherry tomatoes, halved

20 black olives, pitted and
halved

6 canned anchovy fillets,
drained and sliced

1 tbsp chopped fresh oregano

wedges of lemon, to garnish

crusty bread rolls, to serve

for the dressing

4 tbsp extra virgin olive oil

1 tbsp white wine vinegar

1 tbsp lemon juice

1 tbsp chopped fresh flat-leaf
parsley

salt and pepper

anchovy & olive salad

Prepare all the salad ingredients as per ingredients list. To make
the dressing, put all the ingredients, including salt and pepper to
taste, into a small bowl and stir together well.

To assemble the salad, arrange the lettuce leaves in a serving
dish. Scatter the cherry tomatoes on top, followed by the olives,
anchovies, and oregano. Drizzle over the dressing.

Transfer to individual plates, garnish with lemon wedges and
serve with crusty bread rolls.

serves 4

1 cup brown basmati rice

1/2 tsp coriander seeds

2 egg whites, lightly beaten

generous 3/4 cup dry unsweetened coconut

24 raw jumbo shrimp, shelled

1/2 cucumber

4 scallions, thinly sliced lengthwise

1 tsp sesame oil

1 tbsp finely chopped fresh cilantro

coconut shrimp with cucumber salad

Bring a large pan of water to a boil, add the rice, and cook for 25 minutes, or until tender. Drain and keep in a strainer covered with a clean dish towel to absorb the steam.

Meanwhile, soak 8 wooden skewers in cold water for 30 minutes, then drain. Crush the coriander seeds in a mortar with a pestle. Heat a nonstick skillet over medium heat, add the crushed coriander seeds, and cook, turning, until they start to color. Tip onto a plate and set aside.

Put the egg whites into a shallow bowl and the coconut into a separate bowl. Roll each shrimp first in the egg whites, then in the coconut. Thread onto a skewer. Repeat so that each skewer is threaded with 3 coated shrimp.

Preheat the broiler to high. Using a potato peeler, peel long strips from the cucumber to create ribbons, put into a strainer to drain, then toss with the scallions and oil in a bowl, and set aside.

Cook the shrimp under the preheated broiler for 3–4 minutes on each side, or until slightly browned.

Meanwhile, mix the rice with the toasted coriander seeds and fresh cilantro and divide this and the cucumber salad among bowls. Serve with the hot shrimp skewers.

serves 4

12 oz/350 g fresh crabmeat

5 tbsp mayonnaise

2 fl oz/50 ml natural yogurt

4 tsp extra virgin olive oil

4 tsp lime juice

1 scallion, finely chopped

4 tsp finely chopped fresh parsley

pinch of cayenne pepper

1 cantaloupe melon

2 radicchio heads, separated into leaves

fresh parsley sprigs, to garnish

cantaloupe & crab salad

Place the crabmeat in a large bowl and pick over it very carefully to remove any remaining shell or cartilage, but try not to break up the meat.

Put the mayonnaise, yogurt, olive oil, lime juice, scallion, chopped fresh parsley, and cayenne pepper into a separate bowl and mix until thoroughly blended. Fold in the crabmeat.

Cut the melon in half and remove and discard the seeds. Slice into wedges, then cut off the rind with a sharp knife.

Arrange the melon wedges and radicchio leaves on 4 large serving plates, then arrange the crabmeat mixture on top. Garnish with a few sprigs of fresh parsley and serve.

serves 2

2 raw lobster tails

radicchio leaves

fresh dill sprigs, to garnish

for the mayonnaise

1 large lemon

1 large egg yolk

1/2 tsp Dijon mustard

2/3 cup olive oil

1 tbsp chopped fresh dill

salt and pepper

lobster salad

To make the mayonnaise, finely grate half the lemon rind and squeeze the juice. Beat the egg yolk in a small bowl, then beat in the mustard and 1 teaspoon of the lemon juice.

Using a balloon whisk or electric mixer, beat the oil into the egg yolk mixture, drop by drop, until a thick mayonnaise forms. Stir in the lemon rind and 1 tablespoon of the remaining lemon juice.

Season the mayonnaise to taste with salt and pepper and add more lemon juice if desired. Stir in the dill, cover, and let chill in the refrigerator until required.

Bring a large pan of lightly salted water to a boil. Add the lobster tails, return to a boil, and cook for 6 minutes, or until the flesh is opaque and the shells are red. Drain at once and set aside to cool.

Remove the lobster flesh from the shells and cut into bite-size pieces. Arrange the radicchio leaves on individual plates and top with the lobster flesh. Place a spoonful of the lemon-dill mayonnaise on the side. Garnish with dill sprigs and serve.

serves 4

9 oz/250 g live mussels

12 oz/350 g live scallops,
shucked and cleaned

9 oz/250 g prepared squid,
cut into rings and tentacles

1 red onion, halved and
finely sliced

chopped parsley, to garnish

lemon wedges, to serve

for the dressing

4 tbsp extra virgin olive oil

2 tbsp white wine vinegar

1 tbsp lemon juice

1 garlic clove, finely chopped

1 tbsp chopped fresh flat-leaf
parsley

salt and pepper

seafood salad

Clean the mussels by scrubbing or scraping the shells and pulling out any beards that are attached to them. Discard any with broken shells or any that refuse to close when tapped. Put the mussels in a colander and rinse well under cold running water. Put them in a large pan with a little water and cook, covered, over a high heat, shaking the pan occasionally, for 3–4 minutes, or until the mussels have opened. Discard any mussels that remain closed. Strain the mussels, reserving the cooking liquid. Refresh the mussels under cold running water, drain, and set aside.

Return the reserved cooking liquid to the pan and bring to a boil, add the scallops and squid, and cook for 3 minutes. Remove from the heat and drain. Refresh under cold running water and drain again. Remove the mussels from their shells. Put them in a bowl with the scallops and squid and let cool. Cover with plastic wrap and let chill in the refrigerator for 45 minutes.

Divide the seafood among 4 serving plates and top with the onion. Combine all the dressing ingredients in a small bowl, then drizzle over the salad. Garnish with chopped parsley and serve with lemon wedges.

Healthy Salads

serves 4

1¹/3 cups wild rice

3¹/2 cups water

1 each red, yellow, and orange bell peppers, skinned, seeded, and thinly sliced

¹/2 cucumber, halved lengthwise and sliced

1 orange, peeled and pith removed, cubed

3 ripe tomatoes, cut into chunks

1 red onion, very finely chopped

generous handful of chopped flat-leaf parsley

for the dressing

1 clove garlic, crushed

1 tbsp balsamic vinegar

2 tbsp extra virgin olive oil

salt and pepper

wild rice salad with cucumber & orange

Put the wild rice and water into a large pan and bring to a boil. Stir, then cover and simmer for 40 minutes, or until the rice is al dente (firm to the bite). Uncover the rice for the last few minutes of cooking to let any excess water evaporate.

To make the dressing, put the garlic, vinegar, olive oil, and seasoning into a screw-top jar and shake vigorously. Add extra vinegar, oil, or seasoning as required.

Drain the rice and turn into a large bowl. Pour over the dressing and mix in. Then mix in the chopped bell peppers, cucumber, orange, tomatoes, onion, and flat-leaf parsley and serve.

serves 4

1²/₃ cups bean sprouts,
washed and dried

small bunch seedless black
and green grapes, halved

12 unsulfured dried apricots,
halved

¹/₄ cup blanched almonds,
halved

black pepper

for the dressing

1 tbsp walnut oil

1 tsp sesame oil

2 tsp balsamic vinegar

bean sprout, apricot & almond salad

Place the bean sprouts in the bottom of a large salad bowl and sprinkle the grapes and apricots on top.

Place the oils and vinegar in a screw-top jar and shake vigorously to mix. Pour over the salad.

Scatter over the almonds and season with freshly ground black pepper.

serves 4

generous 1 cup quinoa

2^1/$_2$ cups water

10 vine-ripened cherry
tomatoes, halved

3-inch/7.5-cm piece
cucumber, diced

3 scallions, finely chopped

juice of ^{1}/$_2$ lemon

2 tbsp extra virgin olive oil

4 tbsp chopped fresh mint

4 tbsp chopped fresh cilantro

4 tbsp chopped fresh parsley

salt and pepper

tabbouleh

Put the quinoa into a medium-size pan and cover with the water.
Bring to a boil, then reduce the heat, cover, and let simmer over
low heat for 15 minutes. Drain if necessary.

Let the quinoa cool slightly before combining with the remaining
ingredients in a salad bowl. Adjust the seasoning, if necessary,
before serving.

serves 4

2 zucchini, cut into thin sticks

3¹/₂ oz/100 g green beans, cut into thirds

1 green bell pepper, seeded and cut into strips

2 celery stalks, sliced

1 bunch of watercress

for the dressing

scant 1 cup plain yogurt

1 garlic clove, crushed

2 tbsp chopped fresh mint

pepper

zucchini & mint salad

Cook the thin zucchini sticks and beans in a pan of lightly salted water for 7–8 minutes. Drain, rinse under cold running water, and drain again. Let cool completely.

Mix the zucchini and beans with the green bell pepper strips, celery, and watercress in a large serving bowl.

To make the dressing, combine the yogurt, garlic, and mint in a small bowl. Season to taste with pepper.

Spoon the dressing onto the salad and serve immediately.

serves 4-6

6 oz/175 g mixed salad greens, such as spinach, arugula, and curly endive

1 red onion

3 oz/85 g radishes

6 oz/175 g cherry tomatoes

4 oz/115 g cooked beet

10 oz/280 g canned cannellini beans, drained and rinsed

7 oz/200 g canned red kidney beans, drained and rinsed

10$^{1}/_{2}$ oz/300 g canned flageolets, drained and rinsed

scant $^{1}/_{3}$ cup dried cranberries

scant $^{1}/_{2}$ cup roasted cashews

8 oz/225 g feta cheese (drained weight), crumbled

for the dressing

4 tbsp extra virgin olive oil

1 tsp Dijon mustard

2 tbsp lemon juice

1 tbsp chopped fresh cilantro

salt and pepper

three bean salad

Arrange the salad leaves in a salad bowl and reserve.

Thinly slice the onion, then cut in half to form half moons and put into a bowl.

Thinly slice the radishes, cut the tomatoes in half, peel the beet, if necessary, and dice. Add to the onion with the remaining ingredients, except the nuts and cheese.

Put all the ingredients for the dressing into a screw-top jar and shake until blended. Pour over the bean mixture, toss lightly, then spoon on top of the salad leaves.

Scatter over the nuts and cheese and serve immediately.

serves 2

7 oz/200 g buckwheat noodles

9 oz/250 g firm smoked tofu (drained weight)

7 oz/200 g white cabbage, finely shredded

9 oz/250 g carrots, finely shredded

3 scallions, diagonally sliced

1 fresh red chile, seeded and finely sliced into circles

2 tbsp sesame seeds, lightly toasted

for the dressing

1 tsp grated fresh ginger

1 garlic clove, crushed

6 oz/175 g silken tofu (drained weight)

4 tsp tamari (wheat-free soy sauce)

2 tbsp sesame oil

4 tbsp hot water

salt

buckwheat noodle salad with smoked tofu

Cook the noodles in a large pan of lightly salted boiling water according to the package instructions. Drain and refresh under cold running water.

To make the dressing, blend the ginger, garlic, silken tofu, tamari, oil, and water together in a small bowl until smooth and creamy. Season to taste with salt.

Place the smoked tofu in a steamer. Steam for 5 minutes, then cut into thin slices.

Meanwhile, put the cabbage, carrots, scallions, and chile into a bowl and toss to mix. To serve, arrange the noodles on serving plates and top with the carrot salad and slices of tofu. Spoon over the dressing and sprinkle with sesame seeds.

serves 4

large handful of radicchio

large handful of arugula

1 small galia melon

2 ripe avocados

1 tbsp lemon juice

7 oz/200 g fontina cheese,
cut into bite-size pieces

for the dressing

5 tbsp lemon-flavored or
extra virgin olive oil

1 tbsp white wine vinegar

1 tbsp lemon juice

1 tbsp chopped fresh parsley

avocado salad

To make the dressing, mix together the oil, vinegar, lemon juice, and parsley in a small bowl.

Arrange the radicchio and arugula on serving plates. Cut the melon in half, then seed it, and cut the flesh away from the skin. Discard the skin. Slice the melon flesh and arrange it over the salad greens.

Cut the avocados in half and remove and discard the pits and skin. Slice the flesh and brush with lemon juice. Arrange the slices over the melon, then scatter over the cheese. Drizzle over the dressing and serve.

serves 4

6 oz/175 g dried chickpeas or 1½ cups canned, drained and rinsed

2–3 ripe tomatoes, coarsely chopped

1 red onion, thinly sliced

handful of fresh basil leaves, torn

1 lettuce, torn

crusty bread, to serve

for the dressing

1 green chile, seeded and finely chopped

1 garlic clove, crushed

juice of 2 lemons

2 tbsp olive oil

1 tbsp water

black pepper

chickpea & tomato salad

If using dried chickpeas, soak overnight, then boil for 30 minutes, or until soft. Let cool.

Put the chile, garlic, lemon juice, olive oil, water, and black pepper in a screw-top jar and shake vigorously. Taste and add more lemon juice or oil if necessary.

Add the tomatoes, onion, and basil to the chickpeas and mix gently. Pour over the dressing and mix again. Arrange on a bed of lettuce and serve with crusty bread.

serves 4

3 oz/85 g cucumber, cut into batons

6 scallions, halved

2 tomatoes, seeded and each cut into 8 wedges

1 yellow bell pepper, seeded and cut into strips

2 celery stalks, cut into strips

4 radishes, quartered

3 oz/85 g arugula

1 tbsp chopped fresh mint, to garnish (optional)

for the dressing

2 tbsp lemon juice

1 garlic clove, crushed

2/3 cup natural yogurt

2 tbsp olive oil

salt and pepper

salad with garlic dressing

To make the salad, gently mix the cucumber batons, scallions, tomato wedges, yellow bell pepper strips, celery strips, radishes, and arugula in a large serving bowl.

To make the dressing, stir together the lemon juice, garlic, natural yogurt, and olive oil in a small bowl until thoroughly combined. Season with salt and pepper to taste.

Spoon the dressing over the salad and toss to mix. Sprinkle the salad with chopped mint (if using) and serve.

serves 4

1 sweet potato

4 baby carrots, halved

4 tomatoes

4 celery stalks, chopped

8 oz/225 g canned cranberry beans, drained and rinsed

4 oz/115 g mixed salad greens, such as curly endive, arugula, radicchio and looseleaf lettuce

1 tbsp golden raisins

4 scallions, sliced diagonally

for the dressing

2 tbsp lemon juice

1 garlic clove, crushed

5 fl oz/150 ml natural yogurt

2 tbsp olive oil

salt and pepper

sweet potato & bean salad

Peel and dice the sweet potato. Bring a pan of water to a boil over medium heat. Add the sweet potato and cook for 10 minutes, until tender. Drain the potato, transfer to a bowl, and set aside.

Cook the carrots in a separate pan of boiling water for 1 minute. Drain thoroughly and add to the sweet potato. Cut the tops off the tomatoes and scoop out the seeds. Chop the flesh and add to the bowl with the celery and beans. Mix well.

Line a large serving bowl with the mixed salad greens. Spoon the sweet potato and bean mixture on top, then sprinkle with the golden raisins and scallions.

Put all the dressing ingredients, including salt and pepper to taste, in a screw-top jar, screw on the lid and shake until well blended. Pour over the salad and serve.